# Hassle Free Radish C

C000083749

## Simple Delicious Radish Recipes

## Introduction

Welcome to our radish adventure. Whether you decided to join us because you can't live without radishes or you are just discovering your love for radishes. This Hassle – Free Radish Cookbook is definitely the book for you. We all know and agree that radishes are delicious root vegetables, but did you know that they are also filled with nutrients that also provide a wide range of health benefits including:

1. Aiding in nutrition
2. Fighting off viruses such as the flu or common cold
3. And Boosting immunity, to name a few

There are so many things that I could say about the humble radish, but instead of rambling on, I think it will be far more beneficial for us to jump right into the delicious recipes.

## Radish Pine Nut Pesto

This delicious pesto goes well with seafood.

**Serves:** 6

**Time:** 25 mins.

**Ingredients:**

- pepper
- 2 -3 cups radish leaves, chopped
- 1 tsp white sugar
- 3 tbsp parmesan cheese, grated
- 2 tbsp olive oil
- 2 tbsp pine nuts
- salt
- 2 -3 garlic cloves, quartered
- 2 tbsp lemon juice

**Directions:**

1. Add the lemon juice, olive oil, garlic and radish leaves in a food processor and pulse till a thick paste.
2. Add more olive oil if necessary, to bring to your desired consistency.
3. Add the sugar, cheese, nuts, salt and pepper and pulse till well combined.
4. Refrigerate to blend the flavors.

## Simple Radish Chips

Enjoy these chips as a late afternoon snack.
**Serves:** 4
**Time:** 25 mins.

• Radishes, 10-15
• cooking spray, nonstick
• pepper, to taste
• salt, to taste

**Directions:**
1. Set your oven to 375F before doing anything else and lightly, grease a baking sheet.
2. Coat radish slices with cooking spray then season thoroughly.
3. Cook in the oven for about 10 minutes. 4. Flip and cook in the oven for about 5-10 minutes more.

## South American Salsa

This tasty salsa is light, fresh and best served with grilled meats.
**Serves:** 6
**Time:** 10 mins.
**Ingredients:**

- 1 C. radish, chopped medium dice
- 1 C. tomatoes, chopped medium dice
- 1/2 C. cilantro, chopped
- 1/2 C. red onion, chopped
- 2 tbsp fresh lemon juice

• salt ( to taste)

**Directions:**
1. Mix all the Ingredients for the recipe together in a bowl. 2. Serve immediately.

## Russian Summertime Salad

PetersFoodAdventures

Here we have yet another light and tasty salad perfect for summer.

**Serves:**4

**Time:** 15 mins.

**Ingredients:**

**For salad:**

- 10 -12 C. salad greens, torn into bite-sized
- 3/4 C. red radish, cut in 1/16-inch slices
- 1/4 C. green onion, cut in 1/8-inch slices

**For dressing:**

- 1 tbsp cider vinegar
- 1 1/2 tbsp apple juice
- 1 tsp country-style Dijon mustard
- 1 pinch salt
- 1 pinch pepper
- 3 tbsp walnut oil
- 1 pinch sugar (optional)

**Directions:**

1. Place the salad greens, top it with the radish and onions, in a large bowl.
2. Add all the dressing ingredients in a large bowl except for the oil and beat till well combined.
3. Slowly, add the oil, beating continuously till well combined. 4. Place the dressing over the salad and toss to coat well.

# 5-Ingredient Pickles

Serve these unique pickled radishes in your breakfast sandwiches for a tasty twist.

**Serves:** 5

**Time:** 2 hrs. 20 mins.

**Ingredients:**

- 1/4 C. white wine vinegar
- 2 tbsp sugar
- 1 C. carrot, grated
- 1 C. daikon radish, grated
- 1 tbsp salt

1. Mix the salt, carrot and radish in a bowl keep aside for about 10 minutes.
2. Transfer the vegetables mixture into a colander and rinse.
3. Squeeze the vegetables to remove the excess liquid.
4. In a bowl, place the squeezed vegetable mixture, sugar and vinegar and toss to coat. 5. Refrigerate, covered to marinate for about 2 hours.

## Sweet Radishes

Satisfy your sweet tooth with this easy and healthy snack.
**Serves:** 4
**Time:** 25 mins.
**Ingredients:**

• 45 radishes, ends trimmed
• 2 tbsp butter
• 2 tbsp sugar
• 1 tbsp white vinegar
• 1 tsp coarse salt
• 1/4 tsp ground pepper 1. Cut the large radishes in half but leave the small ones whole.

2. In a 12-inch skillet, mix together the radishes, butter, sugar, vinegar, 1 tsp of the salt, pepper and 1 1/2 C. of the water over high heat and bring to a boil. 3. Cook for about 10-15 minutes, stirring occasionally. 4. Serve immediately.

# Chicken with Seoul (Korean Chicken)

The daikon radish provides a delicious side to semi sweet and gazed meats.

**Serves:** 2

**Time:** 40 mins.

**Ingredients:**

- 1/2 tsp chili flakes
- 1 medium daikon radish
- 1 tbsp vegetable oil
- 1 tsp sesame oil
- 1 crushed garlic clove
- 2 boneless chicken legs with thigh

**Cooking Sauce:**

- 1 tbsp sugar
- 1/4 tsp mirin
- 3 tbsp soy sauce
- 2 tbsp sake
- pepper
- 2 C. chicken stock

**Directions:**
1. Cut daikon into 1/2-inch half-moons after peeling it.
2. Cut the chicken in 1-inch pieces.
3. Heat the vegetable oil over high heat. Sauté the chicken and daikon, in a large skillet.
4. Stir in the chili flakes and crushed garlic.
5. Reduce the heat to medium.
6. Add the all the sauce Ingredients and cook, skimming off the fats from the top.
7. When the sauce has been reduced enough, drizzle with the sesame oil. 8. Remove from the heat and serve.

## Silvia's Potluck Dip

This delicious dip will change the way you enjoy chips forever.

**Serves:** 6

**Time:** 40 mins.

**Ingredients:**

- 8 oz. cream cheese ( softened)
- 1/2 C. butter (softened)
- 1/2 tsp celery salt
- 1/8 tsp paprika
- 1/8 tsp red cayenne pepper
- 1/2 tsp Worcestershire sauce
- 1 C. finely chopped red radish
- 1/4 C. finely chopped green onion

**Directions:**

1. Mix all the Ingredients in a bowl.
2. Refrigerate to chill completely. 3. Serve over the rye rounds or crackers.

## Amish Inspired Relish

This radish condiment serves as the finishing touch to any dish.

**Serves:** 12

**Time:** 30 mins.

**Ingredients:**

- 1 lb. radish, julienned
- 1 medium onion, julienned
- 2 tbsp whole allspice
- 1/4 tsp whole cloves
- 1 tsp mustard seeds
- 1 C. white vinegar
- 3/4 C. sugar
- 1/2 tsp salt
- 3/4 C. water

**Directions:**

1. In a bowl, mix together radishes and onions and keep aside.

2. In cheesecloth, place the allspice, cloves and mustard seeds and tie together.
3. In a pan, add the cheesecloth with remaining Ingredients and bring to a boil.
4. Reduce the heat and simmer, uncovered for about 10 minutes.
5. Place the mixture over vegetables and keep aside to steep for about 15 minutes.
6. Transfer into a clean pint jar and keep aside to cool slightly. 7. Cover and refrigerate.

## Hong Kong City Style Radishes

For a small taste of Asian inspired cuisine give this tasty side a go.

**Serves:** 3
**Time:** 1 hr. 5 mins.
**Ingredients:**

- 20 radishes, sliced
- 1 green bell pepper, cut in slivers
- 1 1/2 tbsp soy sauce
- 2 tbsp vinegar

• 1 tbsp sugar

1. Mix all the Ingredients in a bowl. 2. Refrigerate to chill completely before serving.

## Canning Radish

This delicious pickle takes time to infuse the required flavor but with every bite you will see that it is well worth the wait.

**Serves:** 1

**Time:** 8 hrs. 20 mins.

**Ingredients:**

- 2 C. sliced radishes, sliced
- 1 small onion, cut into thin wedges
- 1/2 C. seasoned rice vinegar
- 1/2 C. sugar
- 1 1/2 tsp salt

1. Mix together the radish slices and onions in a container.
2. Add the sugar, salt and vinegar in a bowl. Mix until the sugar has dissolved.
3. Place the dressing over the radish mixture and toss to coat. 4. Covered and refrigerate, for at 8 hours or more, before serving.

# Cream Chives on Pumpernickel

These seasoned radishes pair well with cream cheese and are delicious in these pumpernickel sandwiches.

**Serves:** 1
**Time:** 20 mins.
**Ingredients:**

• radishes, 8, trimmed
• cream cheese, 6 oz.
• butter, 2 tbsp., unsalted
• parsley, 1 tbsp., stems removed
• chives, 1 tsp., snipped
• lemon juice, as needed
• salt, to taste
• black pepper, to taste
• pumpernickel bread, 6 -8 slices, crust removed and cut in squares
• Garnish
• radishes, 4, trimmed
• coarse salt, for garnish

**Directions:**
1. In a food processor, add the radishes and pulse till chopped finely.
2. In a large colander, place the radishes and with the paper towels, squeeze out the excess liquid.
3. Combine your cream cheese and butter then beat till fluffy.
4. Add pepper, salt, lemon juice, chives, parsley and radishes and mix till well combined.
5. Spread the radish mixture over the bread slices evenly.
6. Top with the whole radishes coated with the coarse salt. 7. Refrigerate to chill completely before serving.

# Orange Radish Relish

Serve a dap of this citrusy relish with all your seafood dishes.
**Serves:** 6
**Time:** 1 hr. 30 mins.
**Ingredients:**

- 2 C. radishes, thinly sliced
- 1/2 C. onion, chopped
- 3 tbsp orange juice
- 2 tbsp lime juice
- 2 tbsp fresh cilantro, chopped
- 2 tbsp canola oil
- salt and pepper

**Directions:**
1. Combine all your Ingredients. 2. Cover and refrigerate until chilled then serve.

## Friday Night Radish Curry

This Friday Night Radish Curry is Indian inspired and delicious.
**Serves:** 4
**Time:** 1 hr.
**Ingredients:**

- 2 acorn squash, halved and seeded
- 1 tbsp olive oil
- 1/2 C. diced red bell pepper
- 1/2 C. sliced daikon radish
- 1/4 C. sliced leek
- 1/4 C. diced celery
- 1 jalapeno pepper, diced
- 1 tbsp minced garlic
- 2 C. vegetable stock
- 1 C. brown rice
- 1 C. chopped collard greens
- 1 tbsp curry powder
- 1 1/2 tsp red curry paste

- 1/4 C. chopped walnuts
- 1/2 C. crumbled feta cheese

**Directions:**
1. With a plastic wrap, cover each squash half.
2. Place the cut side of your squash down in a microwave safe dish, and microwave on High for about 12-15 minutes.
3. Remove from the microwave and keep aside the squash wrapped while preparing the filling.
4. In a large skillet, heat the olive oil over medium heat and cook the red bell pepper, radish, leek, celery, jalapeño pepper and garlic for about 10 minutes.
5. Stir in the vegetable stock and rice and simmer, covered for about 45 minutes.
6. Place the greens into the rice mixture and simmer, covered for about 5 minutes.
7. Stir in your walnuts, curry paste and curry powder.
8. Unwrap the squash halves and place into 4 soup bowls, cut sides up.
9. Divide your feta cheese into each side of your squash then top with your rice mixture. 10. Top the rice mixture layer with any leftover feta and serve.

## South-East Asian Rolls

These Asian rolls are super delicious and perfect for all radish lovers.
**Serves:** 4
**Time:** 1 hr.
**Ingredients:**

• Turkey, 1 lb., ground
• 1 tbsp light soy sauce
• Garlic, 1 tsp., minced
• ginger root, 2 tsp., minced
• brown rice, 1 C.
• water, 1 C.
• lettuce, 16 large leaves
• carrots, 1 C., shredded
• green onions, 1 C., thinly sliced
• red bell pepper, 1 C., sliced
• radishes, 1 C., sliced
• soy sauce, 1/3 C.
• water, 1/3 C.
• lemon juice, 3 tbsp.
• garlic, 2 tsp., minced
• ginger root, 1 tbsp., minced
• sugar, 1 tsp.

**Directions:**
1. In a bowl, add the ground turkey, 1 tbsp of the soy sauce, 1 tsp of the minced garlic and 2 tsp of the ginger and mix till well combined.
2. Make 16 equal sized meatballs from the mixture and then roll into ovals.
3. Arrange the balls in a baking sheet in a single layer and refrigerate, covered.
4. In a medium pan, mix together the rice, 2 C. of the water over medium heat and bring to a boil.
5. Switch the heat to low and simmer (about 20 minutes).
6. Set the broiler of your oven and arrange oven rack about 6-inches from the heating element.
7. Line a broiler pan with a piece of the foil.
8. In a serving plate, arrange the red peppers, radishes, scallions, carrots, lettuce, and rice.

9. Combine 1/3 C. of the soy sauce, 1/3 C. of the water, lemon juice, 2 tsp of the garlic, 1 tbsp of the ginger and sugar.

10. Divide the mixture into 4 small dipping bowls. 11. Thread 2 meatballs onto each 10-inch skewer.

12. Arrange the skewers onto the prepared broiler pan.

13. Set under your broiler to cook (about 10-12 minutes, flipping occasionally).

14. Add a lettuce leaf flat in your hand.

15. Place a little rice over lettuce leaf, followed by a meat roll and a few of the vegetables. 16. Roll up and dip in dipping sauce and serve.

## Lone Star Real Ranch Slaw

Add in some radishes to your next slaw and watch the look of awe you get with every bite.

**Serves:** 8

**Time:** 1 hr. 15 mins.

**Ingredients:**

• Mayonnaise, 1 cup
• lime juice, 1 tablespoon
• ground cumin, 1 tablespoon
• cayenne pepper, 1 teaspoon
• salt, 1 teaspoon
• black pepper, 1 teaspoon
• green cabbage, 1 head, medium, rinsed and very thinly sliced
• carrot, 1 large, shredded
• green onions, 2 stalks, sliced
• radishes, 2, sliced

**Directions:**

1. Combine your pepper, salt, cumin, lime juice, and mayonnaise.
2. Add the cabbage, carrot, green onions and radishes and mix till well combined. 3. Refrigerate to chill then serve.

# Advanced Lebanese Salad (Fattoush)

This tasty Lebanese inspired salad will keep you full for hours.
**Serves:** 6
**Time:** 1 hr.
**Ingredients:**

• Lettuce, 6 leaves, chopped
• Cabbage, 3 leaves, chopped
• radishes, 2, small, minced
• cucumber, 1, medium, diced
• red bell pepper, 1, minced
• carrot, 1, shredded
• sweet corn kernels, 1/4 C.
• tomato, 1 large, finely diced
• onion, 1 small, sliced thin
• garlic, 2 cloves, crushed
• parsley, 12 sprigs, minced
• mint, 12 leaves, minced
• olive oil, 1/4 C.
• 1/4 C. pomegranate seeds (optional)
• pomegranate syrup, 1/4 C.
• pita bread, 2 (6 inch), rounds (optional)
• vegetable oil, 2 C., for frying (optional)

**Directions:**
1. Combine your olive oil, mint, parsley, garlic, onion, tomato, corn, carrot, bell pepper, cucumber, radish, cabbage and lettuce then toss to coat well.
2. In a deep-fryer, heat the oil to 350 degrees F and fry the pita breads till golden in color.
3. Transfer the pita breads onto a paper towel lined plate to drain and then crush into small pieces.
4. Serve the salad with a sprinkling of the pita bread pieces.

# Vibrantly Colored Salad

This cucumber and radish salad is light, refreshing and perfect for a hot summer day.

**Serves:** 4
**Time:** 15 mins.
**Ingredients:**

- baby spinach, 6 C., rinsed and dried
- tomatoes, 4, ripe, sliced
- cucumber, 1, English, chopped
- radishes, 10, thinly sliced
- feta cheese, 1/4 C., crumbled
- red bell pepper, 1, seeded, thinly sliced

**Directions:**
1. Combine your ingredients in a large bowl.

2. Top with your favorite dressing and serve.

## Radish Tartine

This delicious Radish Tartine will transport you to modern France with every taste.

**Serves:** 4
**Time:** 30 mins.
**Ingredients:**
**Lemon Aioli:**

- Garlic, 1 clove, sliced
- kosher salt, 1/4 tsp
- lemon juice, 1 tbsp
- lemon zest, 1 tsp
- cayenne pepper, 1 pinch
- mayonnaise, 3/4 C.

### Tartine:

- French bread, 4 slices, thick, day-old
- anchovy fillets, 16, white
- endive, 3/4 C., curly, torn into bite-size pieces
- rainbow carrot strips, 3/4 C., shaved
- radishes, 1/2 C., very thinly sliced
- lemon, 1, juiced
- olive oil, a drizzle
- flowers, 4 edible (optional)
- parsley leaves, 1 tbsp., baby

### Directions:
1. In a bowl, add the garlic and salt and mash till a smooth paste forms.
2. Add mayonnaise, cayenne, lemon zest, and lemon juice then mix till well combined.
3. Toast the bread slices.
4. Spread the lemon aioli over toasted bread slices generously.
5. Place anchovies on top of the aioli, about 4 fillets per tartine.
6. In a bowl, add the olive oil, lemon juice, radish, endive, and carrot strips then gently toss to coat.
7. Arrange the endive on the anchovies, followed by the carrots and radishes.
8. Top with the parsley and flower petals.

## Spicy Radish Salsa

Add a dash of spice to your barbecue dinner with this Spicy Radish Salsa.
**Serves:** 6
**Time:** 15 mins.
**Ingredients:**

- 7 radishes, cut into 1/4-inch chunks
- Cilantro, 1/4 C., chopped
- onion, ¼, diced
- 1 tbsp finely chopped ginger
- 1 tbsp oil
- 1 jalapeno pepper, finely chopped
- 1/2 lime, juiced

**Directions:** 1. In a bowl, mix together all Ingredients and serve.

## Vegetarian Radish Squares

Radish squares make for the perfect side or addition to your next one pot meal.
**Serves:** 6
**Time:** 25 mins.
**Ingredients:**

- 2 (8 oz.) packages refrigerated crescent rolls, unrolled
- 2 (8 oz.) packages cream cheese
- 1 C. mayonnaise
- 1 tsp dried dill weed
- broccoli, 1 head, minced
- cauliflower, 1 head, finely chopped
- radishes, 1 bunch, finely diced
- carrots, 4 jumbo, shredded
- green onions, 1 bunch, chopped
- Swiss cheese, 8 oz., shredded

1 (2.5 oz.) jar imitation bacon bits
**Directions:**
1. Set your oven to preheat to 350F before doing anything else.
2. Press your rolls together to form a single sheet in your baking tray.
3. Set in oven to cook for about 15 minutes.
4. Remove from the oven and keep aside to cool.
5. Mix together the cream cheese and mayonnaise.
6. Place the mayonnaise mixture over each crescent roll evenly.

7. Sprinkle with the dill weed evenly.

8. Place your carrots, radishes, cauliflower and broccoli over the mayonnaise mixture.

9. Top with veggies, followed by the imitation bacon bits.

10. Refrigerate before serving. 11. Cut into squares and serve.

## Radish Summer Spring Rolls

Radish summer rolls are perfect as a summer snack.

**Serves:** 12

**Time:** 4 hrs. 55 mins.

**Ingredients:**

**Pickles:**

- 1 1/4 C. seasoned rice vinegar
- 1/2 C. water
- 2 tbsp white sugar
- 1 tbsp fish sauce
- 1/4 tsp red pepper flakes
- carrots, 2, jumbo, peeled and cut into matchsticks
- daikon radish, ½, peeled and cut into matchsticks

**Steak:**

- low-soy sauce, 3 tbsp
- 1 tbsp white sugar
- 2 tsp minced garlic
- 1 lb. flat iron steaks
- 2 tbsp vegetable oil, or as needed

**Rolls:**

- 6 (8 1/2-inch) rice paper wrappers
- Bibb lettuce, 6 leaves
- cilantro sprigs, 3 C., loosely packed

**Dipping Sauce:**
- 1/4 C. peanut butter
- 1 tsp Sriracha hot sauce

**Directions:**

1. In a glass bowl, add your red pepper flakes, fish sauce, 2 tablespoons of sugar, water and vinegar then mix till the sugar dissolves.

2. Add the carrots and daikon radish.

3. Place a heavy plate over on top to weigh down the vegetables and refrigerate for about 4 hours or overnight.

4. In a shallow baking dish, combine your soy sauce, 1 tbsp of the sugar and

garlic and mix till the sugar dissolves.

5. Add the steak and press down till covered in the marinade completely. 6. Refrigerate for about 4 hours or overnight.

7. In a ridged grill pan, heat the oil over high heat.

8. Remove the steak from marinade and discard the excess marinade.

9. Cook the steak until on grill pan for about 6-10 minutes per side.

10. Transfer your steak onto your cutting board and keep aside to cool.

11. With a sharp knife, cut the steak across the grain into 24 thin slices.

12. Drain the carrot and daikon radishes, reserving 1/2 C. of the pickling liquid.

13. Fill a shallow bowl with the warm water.

14. Dip 1 rice paper sheet in the water for about 5 seconds to soften.

15. Transfer the rice paper sheet onto a smooth surface.

16. Set 2 lettuce leaves over a half of the closest wrapper.

17. Place 2 steak slices over each lettuce leaf half, followed by 1/4 C. of the carrot and daikon pickles and a few cilantro sprigs.

18. Starting with the bottom edge, begin to roll up rice paper sheet tightly around the filling.

19. After 1 roll, fold in the ends like a burrito, then continue to roll. Repeat until done.

20. Cut the rolls diagonally crosswise and arrange on a serving platter.

21. Combine your sriracha, pickling liquid, and peanut butter then whisk until well combined. 22. Serve the rolls alongside the sauce.

## Ottoman Style Lamb

Radish paired with a whole shoulder of lamb serves for a delicious family meal.

**Serves:** 4

**Time:** 3 hrs. 43 mins.

**Ingredients:**

- 1 tbsp kosher salt
- 1 tsp black pepper
- 1 tsp paprika
- 1/4 tsp cayenne pepper
- 4 (10 oz.) lamb shoulder chops
- 1 tbsp olive oil
- 1/3 C. sherry vinegar
- 2 tbsp white sugar
- 4 oil-packed anchovy fillets
- chicken broth, 1 1/2 C.

- rosemary, 2 tsp., minced
- cinnamon, 1/4 tsp.
- breakfast radishes, 2 bunches, rinsed and trimmed
- 5 fresh mint leaves, finely sliced
- 1 tbsp cold butter

**Directions:**
1. Set your oven to 275 degrees F before doing anything else.
2. In a bowl, mix together the salt, pepper, paprika and cayenne pepper.
3. Place lamb chops onto a smooth surface and rub with the seasoning evenly.
4. In large oven-proof skillet, heat the oil over high heat and sear the lamb chops for about 3-4 minutes per side.
5. Transfer the chops into a bowl.
6. Reduce the heat to low.
7. Add the vinegar, sugar and anchovies and cook, stirring and breaking up the anchovies.
8. Switch to medium heat and cook, stirring continuously for about 3 minutes.
9. Stir in the chicken broth and increase the heat to high.
10. Add the rosemary and cinnamon and bring to a boil.
11. Return the browned lamb chops into pan.
12. Arrange the radishes between the chops.
13. Cover then cook for about 1 1/2 hours in the oven.
14. Flip the chops and cook in the oven for about 1 1/2 hours.
15. Flip the chops again and now, set the oven to 425 degrees F.
16. Uncover the skillet and cook in the oven for about 15-20 minutes. 17. Remove the skillet from the oven.
18. With a slotted spoon, transfer lamb chops and radishes into a serving platter.
19. Place pan on stove over medium-high heat and bring the sauce to a simmer.
20. Simmer till the sauce becomes slightly thick, skimming off the fat from the surface.
21. Remove from the heat and immediately, stir in the mint and butter till the butter melts completely.
22. Place the sauce over the lamb chops and radishes and serve.

# 4 Ingredient Hazelnut Salad

This salad can be whipped up in under 10 minutes and is a good option for a late lunch.

**Serves:** 4
**Time:** 5 mins.
**Ingredients:**

- 1 (5 oz.) package prewashed baby arugula
- 4 medium radishes, trimmed and sliced

- 1/2 C. Hidden Valley(R) Original Ranch(R) Avocado Dressing
- 1/4 C. chopped toasted hazelnuts

**Directions:**
1. In 4 salad plates, divide the arugula and radishes.
2. Drizzle 2 tbsp of the dressing over salad in each plate.
3. Serve with a topping of the hazelnuts.

## Creamy Radish and Onion Soup

The addition of radish in this recipe add a tasty earthy flavor to your typical creamed onion soup.

**Serves:** 6

**Time:** 1 hr.

**Ingredients:**

- Butter, 2 tbsp
- onion, 1, large, diced
- potatoes, 2, medium, sliced
- radish greens, 4 C., raw
- chicken broth, 4 C.
- heavy cream, 1/3 C.
- radishes, 5, sliced

**Directions:**

1. Set your butter to melt on medium heat in a large pan then sauté your onion until they are tender.
2. Stir in the potatoes and radish greens.
3. Add the chicken broth and boil.
4. Switch to low heat then simmer for about 30 minutes.
5. Remove the soup mixture from the heat and keep aside to cool slightly.
6. Transfer soup to your blender, then pulse in batches till smooth.
7. Return the mixture to the saucepan.
8. Add heavy cream and cook, stirring continuously till well combined. 9. Serve with the radish slices.

# Crispy Radish Cakes

These radish cakes can be enjoyed as a late snack or a tasty side.
**Serves:** 4
**Time:** 51 mins.
**Ingredients:**

• daikon radish, 1 1/2 C., grated
• salt, 2 tsp
• garlic clove, 1, minced
• red onion, ½, chopped
• egg, 1, beaten
• bread crumbs, Italian seasoned, 1/2 C.
• black pepper, 1/2 tsp
• paprika, 1/2 tsp
• chili-garlic sauce, 1/2 tsp

vegetable oil, 1 1/2 C., for frying
**Directions:**
1. Place the daikon in a bowl, sprinkle with salt then refrigerate for about 30 minutes.
2. Drain the daikon completely.
3. Add the chili garlic sauce, paprika, pepper, bread crumbs, egg, onion and garlic then mix till well combined.
4. Make 8 small round patties from the mixture.
5. Set oil on medium heat then fry the patties for about 3 minutes per side. 6. Transfer the patties onto a paper towel lined plate to drain. Serve.

# Backroad Radishes

These backroad radishes have a slight peppery flavor that pairs well with bitter salads with sweet dressings.

**Serves:** 4

**Time:** 30 mins.

**Ingredients:**

• radishes, 2 bunches, trimmed
• olive oil, extra-virgin, 2 tbsp
• thyme, 1 tsp.
• salt, to taste
• lemon, ½, juiced

1. Set your oven to pre-heat to 450F then prepare a baking sheet with a piece of foil.
2. Cut the radishes into halves.
3. If there are any large radishes, then cut into quarters.
4. In a bowl, add the radishes, olive oil and thyme and toss to coat.
5. Arrange the radishes onto prepared baking sheet and sprinkle with the salt.
6. Cook in the oven for about 15-20 minutes, tossing after every 5 minutes. 7. Serve with a drizzling of the lemon juice.

## Korean Inspired Radish Pickles

These pickled daikon radish cubes pairs well with steak and glazed meats.
**Serves:** 4
**Time:** 25 mins.
**Ingredients:**

- daikon radishes, peeled, 1 1/2 lb.
- red radish, 1 bunch, trimmed, cut in wedges
- kosher salt, 1 tbsp
- rice vinegar, 1/4 C. (not seasoned)
- sugar, 3 tbsp

• ginger, peeled, 1 tbsp, cut in thin matchsticks

1. Cut the daikon in halves lengthwise, then cut crosswise into 1/4-inch-thick slices.
2. In a large bowl, add the daikon, radishes and kosher salt and toss to coat.
3. Keep aside at the room temperature for about 1 hour, stirring occasionally.
4. Drain the radish mixture in a colander and return to bowl. (do not rinse)
5. In the bowl of radish mixture, add the vinegar, sugar and ginger and mix till the sugar dissolves completely.
6. Refrigerate, covered for at least 12 hours, shaking once or twice. 7. This pickle can be preserved in refrigerator for up to 3 weeks.

## Radish Parcel

This delicious parcel is steamed in a packet on the grill to provide you with a satisfying main.

**Serves:** 6
**Time:** 35 mins.
**Ingredients:**

• radishes, 20 oz., sliced
• garlic, 2 cloves, minced
• butter, 2 tbsp, diced
• ice, 1 cube
• salt and pepper to taste

1. Set your grill for high heat.
2. Place the ice, butter, garlic and radishes onto a large double layer of the foil piece.
3. Sprinkle with the salt and pepper and fold the foil tightly around the radish mixture to seal.
4. Arrange the foil packet over the grill grate. 5. Cook the foil packet on the grill for about 20 minutes.

## South Salinas Slaw

This South Salinas Slaw is vibrant, colorful and tasty.

**Serves:** 10

**Time:** 10 mins.

**Ingredients:**

- 4 C. shredded radishes
- 2 C. chopped yellow peppers
- 1 1/2 C. shredded carrots
- 1/2 C. white wine vinegar
- 4 tsp sugar
- 1 tbsp chopped fresh dill
- 1 tbsp mustard oil
- salt and pepper

1. Mix together the radishes, peppers and carrots.
2. Combine your remaining Ingredients in another bowl and beat till well combined.
3. Place the dressing over the slaw and toss to coat well. 4. Serve immediately.

## Conclusion

That's it! I hope you enjoyed all 30 simple delicious radish recipes featured in this Hassle – Free Radish Cookbook. The humble radish is such a versatile ingredient, hopefully this cookbook was able to introduce you to some new and exciting recipes.

If you enjoyed what you read, please drop me a review on Amazon so that I can fully understand your thoughts.

Printed in Great Britain
by Amazon